THE SEVERED MOON

A YEAR-LONG
JOURNAL OF MAGIC

LEIGH BARDUGO

[Imprint]
MAKE YOUR MARK

NEW YORK

LEIGH BARDUGO is a #1 *New York Times*—bestselling author and the creator of the Grishaverse, which has sold over two million copies and includes the Shadow and Bone Trilogy, the Six of Crows Duology, *The Language of Thorns*, and *King of Scars*. leighbardugo.com

[Imprint]
MAKE YOUR MARK

A part of Macmillan Publishing Group, LLC
175 Fifth Avenue, New York, NY 10010

Library of Congress Cataloging-in-Publication Data is available.

ISBN 978-1-250-20774-6 (hardcover)

Our books may be purchased in bulk for promotional, educational, or business use. Please contact your local bookseller or the Macmillan Corporate and Premium Sales Department at (800) 221-7945 ext. 5442 or by email at MacmillanSpecialMarkets@macmillan.com.

Book design and illustrations by Ellen Duda

Imprint logo designed by Amanda Spielman

First edition, 2019

1 3 5 7 9 10 8 6 4 2

fiercereads.com

A peasant can become a queen,
a pauper rise to prince,
but steal this book and you'll become
a thief never heard of since.

JUST AS THE MOON WAXES AND WANES, inspiration and creativity can ebb and flow according to what we encounter in our daily lives. This journal is meant to help you navigate those cycles of drought and plenty to find a more constant wellspring for your most powerful creative self.

Try to write in this journal every day. It should be both a refuge and a guide. As a refuge, it is a safe and private place to explore your thoughts about the world outside and the magic within. As a guide, it will lead the way to finding more sources of inspiration and creative energy.

Each page has a quotation, a question, or a creative prompt for you to consider—some serious, some playful, many thematically linked. You should feel free to skip ahead or return to those that speak to you at different times. There are no rules for how you respond to these prompts and quotes. You can address them directly, or you can simply write down what they conjure in your mind, how they make you feel, or what they suggest to you about your own life.

I recommend writing in this journal at a consistent time each day. That may be at night when all is still, or in the morning when the day is fresh. Find the time that works best for you.

WE LEARN TO HOLD OUR HEADS AS IF WE WEAR CROWNS.
WE LEARN TO WRING MAGIC FROM THE ORDINARY.

DATE

Describe something in your life that others might view
as ordinary but that you experience as magical.

_____

_____

_____

_____

_____

_____

_____

_____

_____

_____

_____

_____

_____

_____

_____

_____

_____

_____

_____

_____

DATE _____

Tell the story of the most magical day or experience of your life so far.

DATE _____

AROUND THE THICK FUR OF HIS RUFF HE WORE A LARIAT
OF GOLD AND RUBIES, AND THE TWISTING HORNS THAT ROSE
FROM HIS HEAD WERE MARKED WITH RIDGES THAT
GLOWED AS IF LIT FROM WITHIN BY SECRET FIRE.

DATE _____

How do you choose to ornament yourself?
Does it change from day to day?

What stories do you tell through your attire?
Are those stories true?

_____

_____

_____

_____

_____

_____

_____

_____

_____

_____

_____

_____

_____

_____

_____

_____

_____

_____

_____

_____

_____

_____

DATE _____

Describe a garment you would like to
wear that would give you power.

I LOOKED UP AT THE STAR-FILLED SKY. THE NIGHT WAS VELVETY BLACK AND STREWN WITH JEWELS. THE HUNGER STRUCK ME SUDDENLY. *I WANT THEM*, I THOUGHT. ALL THAT LIGHT, ALL THAT POWER. *I WANT IT ALL.*

DATE _____

If you could choose and name your own
constellation, what would it be? Tell its story.

What kind of power do you associate with the night sky?
How could it work for you?

_____

_____

_____

_____

_____

_____

_____

_____

_____

_____

_____

_____

_____

_____

_____

_____

_____

_____

_____

_____

DATE_____

"WHAT NONSENSE! OF COURSE THAT'S NOT HOW THE STORY ENDS." THEN SHE WOUND THE STORY TIGHT AND LET IT UNSPOOL ANEW.

∞ ∞

DATE _____

Is there a story in your life you would
like to rewrite? Tell it here.

_____

_____

_____

_____

_____

_____

_____

_____

_____

_____

_____

_____

_____

_____

_____

_____

_____

_____

_____

_____

_____

_____

DATE_____

How would today's story look different
if you could rewrite it?

_____

_____

_____

_____

_____

_____

_____

_____

_____

_____

_____

_____

_____

_____

_____

_____

_____

_____

DATE_____

OUTSIDE, THE WIND HOWLED. IT WAS LESS THE BAYING OF A BEAST THAN THE HIGH, WILD LAUGH OF AN OLD FRIEND, DRIVING THEM ON. THE WIND DID WHAT SHE WILLED IT, HAD SINCE SHE WAS A CHILD.

DATE

Describe the most powerful natural
event you've experienced.

_____

_____

_____

_____

_____

_____

_____

_____

_____

_____

_____

_____

_____

_____

_____

_____

_____

_____

_____

DATE_____

Describe an outdoor space that you have visited or wish to visit and that you consider to be a special source of creative energy. What symbol of that place can you incorporate into your daily life?

_____

_____

_____

_____

_____

_____

_____

_____

_____

_____

_____

_____

_____

_____

_____

_____

_____

_____

_____

DATE _____

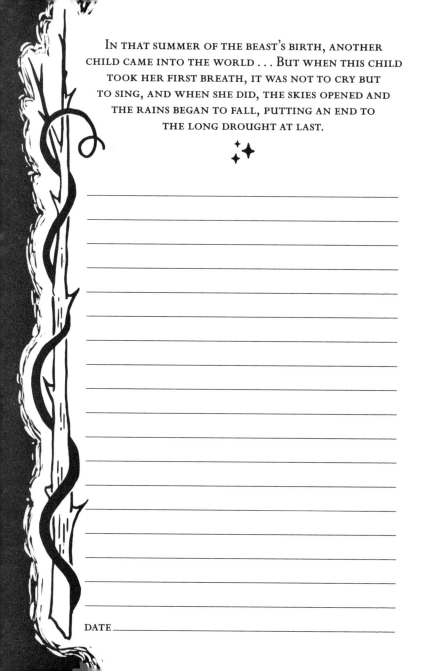

IN THAT SUMMER OF THE BEAST'S BIRTH, ANOTHER
CHILD CAME INTO THE WORLD . . . BUT WHEN THIS CHILD
TOOK HER FIRST BREATH, IT WAS NOT TO CRY BUT
TO SING, AND WHEN SHE DID, THE SKIES OPENED AND
THE RAINS BEGAN TO FALL, PUTTING AN END TO
THE LONG DROUGHT AT LAST.

DATE

Describe how your personality does or
does not match your astrological sign.

_____

_____

_____

_____

_____

_____

_____

_____

_____

_____

_____

_____

_____

_____

_____

_____

_____

_____

_____

_____

DATE_____

Write your own horoscope for the day to come.

DATE

SONG WAS NOT JUST A FRIVOLITY THEN, SOMETHING
MEANT TO ENTERTAIN OR LURE SAILORS TO THEIR
DOOM ... MAGIC FLOWED THROUGH ALL OF THEM,
A SONG NO MORTAL COULD HEAR.

DATE_____

What kind of power do you draw from music?

If you could be proficient in any instrument,
what would it be and why?

_____

_____

_____

_____

_____

_____

_____

_____

_____

_____

_____

_____

_____

_____

_____

_____

_____

_____

DATE_____

HER TONGUE WAS FORKED; HER EYES GLOWED
LIKE OPALS, AND HER HAIR TWINED IN SERPENTS OF
FLAME THAT LICKED AT THE AIR AROUND HER
IN RIBBONS OF ORANGE AND GOLD.

DATE

Describe your monster self.
What would it look like and what powers would it have?

❖ 🌿 ❖

_____

_____

_____

_____

_____

_____

_____

_____

_____

_____

_____

_____

_____

_____

_____

_____

_____

_____

_____

_____

DATE _____

Describe a time when you wished to be feared.

"TELL ME A TALE THAT CAN MAKE ME FEEL MORE THAN ANGER, AND IF YOU MANAGE IT, I MAY LET YOU LIVE."

_____
_____
_____
_____
_____
_____
_____
_____
_____
_____
_____
_____
_____
_____
_____
_____
_____
_____
_____
_____
_____

DATE_____

Is anger useful for creativity? Why or why not?

_____

_____

_____

_____

_____

_____

_____

_____

_____

_____

_____

_____

_____

_____

_____

_____

_____

_____

_____

_____

_____

DATE_____

Think of a time when you were very angry. What kind of story would you have wanted to hear? Tell that story here.

_____

_____

_____

_____

_____

_____

_____

_____

_____

_____

_____

_____

_____

_____

_____

_____

_____

_____

_____

_____

DATE_____

SHE HAD A VISION OF GOLDEN FIELDS BENEATH A
CLOUDLESS SKY, A CLAPBOARD HOUSE PROTECTED FROM
THE WIND BY A LINE OF RED OAKS. SOMEPLACE SAFE.

DATE _____

What places represent safety to you?

_____

_____

_____

_____

_____

_____

_____

_____

_____

_____

_____

_____

_____

_____

_____

_____

_____

_____

_____

_____

DATE _____

How do you provide a sense
of safety or comfort for others?

_____

_____

_____

_____

_____

_____

_____

_____

_____

_____

_____

_____

_____

_____

_____

_____

_____

_____

_____

_____

DATE _____

THE BLOSSOMS GLOWED LIKE
A CONSTELLATION IN HER HAND.

_____

_____

_____

_____

_____

_____

_____

_____

_____

_____

_____

_____

_____

_____

_____

_____

_____

_____

_____

_____

_____

DATE _____

If you have favorite flowers, do you favor
them for their appearance or for their scent?
What emotions do they evoke in you?

DATE

Do you enjoy receiving flowers as a gift or an apology?
Why?

_____
_____
_____
_____
_____
_____
_____
_____
_____
_____
_____
_____
_____
_____
_____
_____
_____
_____
_____
_____
_____

DATE_____

What kind of new flower would you create
if you could dream or wish one into being?

HE THREW BACK HIS HEAD AND HOWLED, THE SOUND
SHAKING THE LEAVES ON THE TREES . . . "THERE IS BUT ONE
RULE IN MY WOOD," HE GROWLED. "SPEAK TRUTH."

DATE _____

Is it always best to speak the perfect truth?
Why or why not?

When was the last time you were tempted to be untruthful?

_____

_____

_____

_____

_____

_____

_____

_____

_____

_____

_____

_____

_____

_____

_____

_____

_____

_____

_____

_____

DATE _____

WHAT GAVE HER STRENGTH THEN? WE CANNOT KNOW
FOR SURE. THAT CONTRARY THING INSIDE HER? THAT HARD
STONE OF RAGE THAT ALL LONELY GIRLS POSSESS?

DATE_____

What power can be found in solitude?

_____

_____

_____

_____

_____

_____

_____

_____

_____

_____

_____

_____

_____

_____

_____

_____

_____

_____

_____

_____

DATE_____

Describe a time you chose to be alone and explain why.

SO I BECAME A HERMIT, AT LEAST FOR A TIME. EVENTUALLY, OF COURSE, PEOPLE SOUGHT ME OUT, EAGER TO LEARN MY SECRETS . . . WE ARE ALWAYS DRAWN TO THE LURE OF POWER, NO MATTER THE COST.

_____

_____

_____

_____

_____

_____

_____

_____

_____

_____

_____

_____

_____

_____

_____

_____

_____

_____

_____

_____

_____

DATE _____

Tell a real or imagined story of discovering a place
that others would prefer to keep secret.

What kinds of knowledge would you most like to unlock?

_____
_____
_____
_____
_____
_____
_____
_____
_____
_____
_____
_____
_____
_____
_____
_____
_____
_____
_____
_____
_____

DATE_____

IT WAS LIKE STANDING IN THE HOLLOWED OUT
TRUNK OF A MASSIVE TREE, SOMETHING LONG
DEAD AND HOWLING WITH ECHOES.

What is a memory you would like to lay to rest?

_____

_____

_____

_____

_____

_____

_____

_____

_____

_____

_____

_____

_____

_____

_____

_____

_____

_____

_____

_____

DATE_____

Take a moment to close your eyes and imagine being alone in a forest. Look around. Describe what you see.

_____

_____

_____

_____

_____

_____

_____

_____

_____

_____

_____

_____

_____

_____

_____

_____

_____

_____

_____

DATE _____

. . . AT ITS CENTER LAY A POOL, NEARLY PERFECT IN
ITS ROUNDNESS, ITS SURFACE SMOOTH AS HIGHLY
POLISHED GLASS, REFLECTING THE SKY SO PURELY
THAT IT LOOKED AS IF ONE COULD STEP INTO IT AND
FALL STRAIGHT THROUGH THE CLOUDS.

✦

DATE _____

What is the most important thing you see in a reflection?

DATE _____

Today or tomorrow, find your reflection in a cup of tea or a still pool. Describe what you see.

_____

_____

_____

_____

_____

_____

_____

_____

_____

_____

_____

_____

_____

_____

_____

_____

_____

_____

_____

DATE_____

THEY OPENED THE CHARM AND LOOKED THROUGH IT:
A SMALL GOLD BUTTON, DRIED HERBS, AND ASHES.
WHATEVER MAGIC MIGHT HAVE WORKED INSIDE IT
WAS INVISIBLE TO THEIR EYES.

DATE

Describe a charm you have carried or would like to carry.
Write a story about where you acquired it.

If you could design a charm of protection,
what would it ward against?

SHE LEARNED WHICH HERBS WERE VALUABLE AND
WHICH WERE DANGEROUS, AND WHICH HERBS WERE
VALUABLE BECAUSE THEY WERE DANGEROUS.

_____

_____

_____

_____

_____

_____

_____

_____

_____

_____

_____

_____

_____

_____

_____

_____

_____

_____

_____

_____

DATE _____

First thing in the morning, try smelling an herb, spice, plant, or flower you are drawn to—common herbs like mint, rosemary, and lavender can all have powerful effects. Did it change your day?

✦✦

_____

_____

_____

_____

_____

_____

_____

_____

Right before you go to sleep, smell an herb, spice, plant, or flower you are drawn to. Did it influence your dreams?

_____

_____

_____

_____

_____

_____

_____

_____

DATE_____

"YOU WILL WEAR BLUE SUMMER SILKS AND EAT
WHITE NECTARINES, AND SLEEP IN A PROPER BED."

DATE

How do you define luxury?
What are your favorite personal luxuries?

_____

_____

_____

_____

_____

_____

_____

_____

_____

_____

_____

_____

_____

_____

_____

_____

_____

_____

_____

_____

_____

_____

DATE _____

If you could pluck any luxury item from a dream,
what would it be?

_____
_____
_____
_____
_____
_____
_____
_____
_____
_____
_____
_____
_____
_____
_____
_____
_____
_____
_____
_____
_____

DATE_____

"NO MOURNERS, NO FUNERALS."
ANOTHER WAY OF SAYING GOOD LUCK.

DATE _____

Are there any rituals you believe can bring you good luck? What rituals have you seen others perform to ward off bad luck?

_____

_____

_____

_____

_____

_____

_____

_____

_____

_____

_____

_____

_____

_____

_____

_____

_____

_____

_____

_____

DATE_____

Describe an occurrence in your life that you or others have attributed to good or bad luck.

_____

_____

_____

_____

_____

_____

_____

_____

_____

_____

_____

_____

_____

_____

_____

_____

_____

_____

_____

DATE_____

Do you have a personal motto?
If not, think about what that motto should be.

_____

_____

_____

_____

_____

_____

_____

_____

_____

_____

_____

_____

_____

_____

_____

_____

_____

_____

_____

DATE _____

HOW EASILY PRINCES PLAYED. HOW EASILY THEY
SPOKE OF DREAMS THEY HAD NO BUSINESS OFFERING.

DATE _____

Do you usually remember your dreams? If you could choose
something to dream of tonight, what would it be?

_____
_____
_____
_____
_____
_____
_____
_____
_____
_____
_____
_____
_____
_____
_____
_____
_____
_____
_____

DATE _____

What was the last dream that felt real to you?

I LOOKED INTO THE STAG'S DARK EYES AND
KNEW THE FEEL OF THE EARTH BENEATH HIS STEADY
HOOVES, THE SMELL OF PINE IN HIS NOSTRILS,
THE POWERFUL BEAT OF HIS HEART.

DATE

What does it mean for an animal
to be wild rather than tame?

Name an animal or creature for which you feel
a special affinity and explain why.

_____

_____

_____

_____

_____

_____

_____

_____

_____

_____

_____

_____

_____

_____

_____

_____

_____

_____

_____

DATE_____

If you could take the form of another animal, what would it be and what would you do in this new form?

_____

_____

_____

_____

_____

_____

_____

_____

_____

_____

_____

_____

_____

_____

_____

_____

_____

_____

_____

DATE _____

AND THEN SHE SMELLED IT, HOT AND SWEET,
A FRAGRANT CLOUD THAT SINGED THE EDGES
OF HER NOSTRILS: BURNING SUGAR.

What fragrance would draw you into a room? Why?

Is there a fragrance you personally dislike that others generally consider pleasant, or vice versa?

_____

_____

_____

_____

_____

_____

_____

_____

_____

_____

_____

_____

_____

_____

_____

_____

_____

_____

_____

DATE _____

Describe the scents you associate with
home, work, and relaxation.

If you could create a personal fragrance,
what would it smell like?

_____

_____

_____

_____

_____

_____

_____

_____

_____

_____

_____

_____

_____

_____

_____

_____

_____

_____

_____

_____

DATE _____

IT FELT LIKE SOMETHING THAT WAS MEANT TO BE KEPT SECRET, A NEW SEED THAT MIGHT GROW TO SOMETHING EXTRAORDINARY IF IT WASN'T FORCED TO BLOOM TOO SOON.

DATE _____

What do you dream of that you haven't told anyone about?

_____
_____
_____
_____
_____
_____
_____
_____
_____
_____
_____
_____
_____
_____
_____
_____
_____
_____
_____
_____
_____

DATE _____

Are you good at keeping secrets?
Why or why not?

_____

_____

_____

_____

_____

_____

_____

_____

_____

_____

_____

_____

_____

_____

_____

_____

_____

_____

_____

_____

_____

_____

DATE _____

What is the danger in forcing something to bloom too soon?

THE OX FEELS THE YOKE, BUT DOES THE BIRD FEEL THE WEIGHT OF ITS WINGS?

DATE

Describe a dream of flight. Do you have wings?
Where do you travel?

_____

_____

_____

_____

_____

_____

_____

_____

_____

_____

_____

_____

_____

_____

_____

_____

_____

_____

_____

_____

DATE_____

In the past, people believed that fortunes could be read in the movements of birds. What bird might bring you good fortune? What story would it tell?

IT TOOK YEARS FOR THE KING TO COMPLETE THE
LABYRINTH, AND HALF THE WORKMEN TASKED
WITH ITS CONSTRUCTION WERE LOST WITHIN
ITS WALLS AND NEVER HEARD FROM AGAIN.

DATE _____

If you had a private maze or labyrinth,
what would it look like and what would be at its center?

∞ 🜨 ∞

_____

_____

_____

_____

_____

_____

_____

_____

_____

_____

_____

_____

_____

_____

_____

_____

_____

_____

_____

_____

DATE _____

When you're trying to solve a difficult
problem, where do you begin and why?

_____

_____

_____

_____

_____

_____

_____

_____

_____

_____

_____

_____

_____

_____

_____

_____

_____

_____

_____

_____

DATE _____

THEY PLAY AT MAGIC, READ THE STARS, THROW BONES.
BUT IT'S BEST NOT TO SHOW THEM REAL POWER.

What is real power?

_____

_____

_____

_____

_____

_____

_____

_____

_____

_____

_____

_____

_____

_____

_____

_____

_____

_____

_____

_____

_____

DATE_____

If you could choose a magical gift
or power, what would it be?

_____

_____

_____

_____

_____

_____

_____

_____

_____

_____

_____

_____

_____

_____

_____

_____

_____

_____

_____

_____

DATE _____

What do you think is your own current greatest power?
What is a concrete way you can encourage this power?

_____

_____

_____

_____

_____

_____

_____

_____

_____

_____

_____

_____

_____

_____

_____

_____

_____

_____

_____

DATE_____

SHE WAS TERRIFYING IN HER BEAUTY,
BRIGHT LIKE A DEVOURING STAR.

DATE _____

What can make beauty terrifying?

_____

_____

_____

_____

_____

_____

_____

_____

_____

_____

_____

_____

_____

_____

_____

_____

_____

_____

_____

_____

_____

_____

DATE _____

How do you personally define beauty?

_____
_____
_____
_____
_____
_____
_____
_____
_____
_____
_____
_____
_____
_____
_____
_____
_____
_____
_____
_____
_____

DATE _____

When do you feel most beautiful?

You see, some people are born with a piece of night inside, and that hollow place can never be filled—not with all the good food or sunshine in the world.

DATE

Describe an instance when you hungered for
something but did not receive it.

BUT AT NIGHT, THE BARN BECAME A HOLLOW SHELL, WAITING FOR SOME TERRIBLE CREATURE TO FILL IT— SOME CUNNING THING THAT MIGHT LET THE DOORS BLOW OPEN TO LURE A FOOLISH BOY.

DATE _____

What kind of vengeful spirits can you
imagine inhabiting our world?

❖ 🌿 ❖

_____

_____

_____

_____

_____

_____

_____

_____

_____

_____

_____

_____

_____

_____

_____

_____

_____

_____

_____

_____

DATE _____

How would you protect yourself from a spiteful entity?

THE BEAST MIGHT SHOUT AND SNARL, AND HE MIGHT
WELL DEVOUR HER, BUT HE'D AT LEAST BEEN
INTERESTED ENOUGH TO LISTEN TO HER SPEAK.

DATE

Do you like the company of those with strong opinions?
Why or why not?

_____

_____

_____

_____

_____

_____

_____

_____

_____

_____

_____

_____

_____

_____

_____

_____

_____

_____

_____

_____

DATE _____

Do you prefer to listen or to speak?
Does this preference change with the company you keep?

DATE _____

There are many stories of human beings trapped in the shapes of beasts. What do you think it means to "become a beast"?

_____

_____

_____

_____

_____

_____

_____

_____

_____

_____

_____

_____

_____

_____

_____

_____

_____

_____

_____

_____

DATE _____

THEY SANG A LULLABY LIKE THE ONES THEIR MOTHER HAD SUNG WHEN THEY WERE YOUNGER, AND SURE ENOUGH, AFTER A LONG WHILE, THE SPIRIT QUIETED—AND AFTER A LONGER WHILE, THE SPIRIT SPOKE.

❖

DATE _____

What is a song or story that brought you
comfort when you were younger?

_____
_____
_____
_____
_____
_____
_____
_____
_____
_____
_____
_____
_____
_____
_____
_____
_____
_____
_____
_____
_____

DATE _____

Is there a song that you believe holds
special significance or power for you now?

_____

_____

_____

_____

_____

_____

_____

_____

_____

_____

_____

_____

_____

_____

_____

_____

_____

_____

DATE_____

THEY CRIED OUT FOR LOVE POTIONS AND UNTRACEABLE
POISONS. THEY BEGGED TO BE MADE BEAUTIFUL, HEALTHY, RICH.

DATE

What kinds of spells do you think would
be most in demand today? Why?

_____

_____

_____

_____

_____

_____

_____

_____

_____

_____

_____

_____

_____

_____

_____

_____

_____

_____

_____

DATE_____

What spell would you most like to be able to perform?
Describe it.

Are there spells you think shouldn't be performed at all?
Why or why not?

_____

_____

_____

_____

_____

_____

_____

_____

_____

_____

_____

_____

_____

_____

_____

_____

_____

_____

_____

DATE_____

SHE DREAMED SHE STOOD AT THE CENTER OF THE
HEDGE MAZE WEARING A MANTLE OF FIRE, PARALYZED,
UNABLE TO DO ANYTHING BUT BURN.

DATE _____

Describe a recurring anxiety dream or nightmare.

_____

_____

_____

_____

_____

_____

_____

_____

_____

_____

_____

_____

_____

_____

_____

_____

_____

_____

_____

DATE _____

What actions would you like
to be able to take in your dreams?

Rewrite the narrative of your worst dream
to provide a more positive outcome.

_____

_____

_____

_____

_____

_____

_____

_____

_____

_____

_____

_____

_____

_____

_____

_____

_____

_____

_____

_____

DATE_____

ON THE EDGE OF THE WOODS, THE TOWNSPEOPLE
BUILT CROOKED ALTARS—CAREFUL STACKS OF
PAINTED ICONS, BURNT-DOWN PRAYER CANDLES,
LITTLE PILES OF FLOWERS AND BEADS.

DATE

If you were to choose a token that
represents you, what would it be? Why?

_____

_____

_____

_____

_____

_____

_____

_____

_____

_____

_____

_____

_____

_____

_____

_____

_____

_____

_____

DATE_____

What do you most like to receive from others?
What do you most like to provide for yourself?

DATE _____

What is your favorite gift you received as a child?
As an adult?

_____

_____

_____

_____

_____

_____

_____

_____

_____

_____

_____

_____

_____

_____

_____

_____

_____

_____

_____

_____

_____

DATE_____

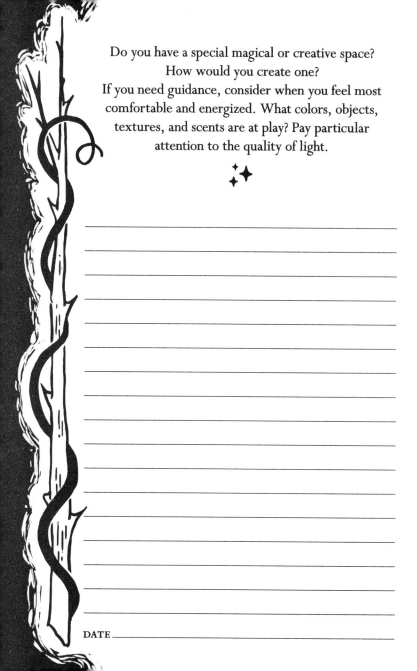

Do you have a special magical or creative space?
How would you create one?
If you need guidance, consider when you feel most
comfortable and energized. What colors, objects,
textures, and scents are at play? Pay particular
attention to the quality of light.

✦

DATE_____

WHO DIDN'T WANT TO THINK FATE HAD A PLAN
FOR HIM, THAT HIS HURTS AND FAILURES HAD JUST
BEEN THE PROLOGUE TO A GRANDER TALE?

_____

_____

_____

_____

_____

_____

_____

_____

_____

_____

_____

_____

_____

_____

_____

_____

_____

_____

_____

_____

_____

DATE _____

Do you believe in fate?
When has that opinion been challenged?

_____

_____

_____

_____

_____

_____

_____

_____

_____

_____

_____

_____

_____

_____

_____

_____

_____

_____

_____

_____

_____

DATE _____

Do you think people get what they deserve?
Why or why not?

❖ 🌿 ❖

_____

_____

_____

_____

_____

_____

_____

_____

_____

_____

_____

_____

_____

_____

_____

_____

_____

_____

_____

_____

DATE _____

THERE WAS NO WAY OF KNOWING WHICH WAY HOME
MIGHT BE. ALL AROUND HER THERE WAS SILENCE,
BROKEN ONLY BY THE HOWL OF THE RISING WIND . . .

DATE

Does the place where you live feel like home to you?
Why or why not?

_____

_____

_____

_____

_____

_____

_____

_____

_____

_____

_____

_____

_____

_____

_____

_____

_____

_____

_____

_____

_____

DATE_____

How do your memories of childhood
affect your definition of home?

Write a story about finding home.

_____

_____

_____

_____

_____

_____

_____

_____

_____

_____

_____

_____

_____

_____

_____

_____

_____

_____

_____

_____

_____

DATE_____

"WANTING IS WHY PEOPLE GET UP IN THE MORNING.
IT GIVES THEM SOMETHING TO DREAM OF AT NIGHT."

DATE

What is something you desire each morning
when you awake?

_____

_____

_____

_____

_____

_____

_____

_____

_____

_____

_____

_____

_____

_____

_____

_____

_____

_____

_____

_____

DATE _____

Which of your desires drives you the most?

THERE WAS NO COFFEE TO BE HAD SO THEY ORDERED TEA
AND LITTLE GLASSES OF CLEAR *BRÄNNVIN* THAT BURNED
GOING DOWN BUT HELPED TO KEEP THEM WARM AS A WIND
PICKED UP, STIRRING THE SILVERY RIBBONS TIED TO
THE ASH BOUGHS LINING THE STREET BELOW.

✦

_____

_____

_____

_____

_____

_____

_____

_____

_____

_____

_____

_____

_____

_____

_____

_____

_____

_____

_____

_____

DATE_____

What taste or flavor makes you happiest?

What food do you associate with childhood?

DATE

What is something you like a little but
would not want to eat a lot of?

SHE KNEW THE IDEA OF FIRE. SHE'D BEEN TAUGHT
ABOUT IT, SUNG THE WORD. BUT *SEEING* IT—SO CLOSE
AND SO ALIVE . . . IT WAS LIKE HAVING A LITTLE
SUN TO KEEP ALL FOR HERSELF.

DATE

Describe a fire—a campfire, a kitchen fire,
a wildfire, a candle burning—and its personality.

What power related to fire would you like to have?

_____

_____

_____

_____

_____

_____

_____

_____

_____

_____

_____

_____

_____

_____

_____

_____

_____

_____

_____

_____

_____

_____

DATE_____

SHE WOULD FIGHT FOR HIM, BUT SHE COULD NOT
HEAL HIM. SHE WOULD NOT WASTE HER LIFE TRYING.

DATE _____

Describe someone in your life you wish you could heal.
Write to that person here.

_____

_____

_____

_____

_____

_____

_____

_____

_____

_____

_____

_____

_____

_____

_____

_____

_____

_____

_____

_____

_____

DATE_____

OUR POWER CONNECTS US TO LIFE IN WAYS ORDINARY PEOPLE CAN NEVER UNDERSTAND, HER TEACHER HAD SAID. THAT'S WHY USING OUR GIFT MAKES US STRONGER INSTEAD OF DEPLETING US.

DATE _____

What gifts do you have that you feel stronger after using?

_____
_____
_____
_____
_____
_____
_____
_____
_____
_____
_____
_____
_____
_____
_____
_____
_____
_____
_____
_____
_____

DATE_____

What gifts do you use that leave you feeling drained?

THE SUN SANK LOWER, SETTING EVERY POOL ALIGHT,
TURNING THE VALLEY INTO A CRUCIBLE.

DATE

When was the last time you watched a sun rise or set?
How do you remember it?

_____

_____

_____

_____

_____

_____

_____

_____

_____

_____

_____

_____

_____

_____

_____

_____

_____

_____

_____

_____

DATE _____

Observe the next sunset. Describe what you saw and felt.

_____

_____

_____

_____

_____

_____

_____

_____

Observe the next sunrise.
Describe what you saw and felt.

_____

_____

_____

_____

_____

_____

_____

_____

_____

DATE _____

SHE KNEW FROM STORIES THAT YOU
MUST NOT EAT AT A WITCH'S TABLE.

What does it mean to be a witch?

_____

_____

_____

_____

_____

_____

_____

_____

_____

_____

_____

_____

_____

_____

_____

_____

_____

_____

_____

DATE _____

What is powerful about sharing a meal with someone?

Who would you never sit down to dine with?
What food would you be afraid to eat?

_____

_____

_____

_____

_____

_____

_____

_____

_____

_____

_____

_____

_____

_____

_____

_____

_____

_____

_____

DATE_____

How would you set a magical table?

AND SO MANY STARS—A GLITTERING, TANGLED MASS
THAT SEEMED CLOSE ENOUGH TO TOUCH. I LET THEIR
LIGHT FALL OVER ME LIKE A BALM, GRATEFUL FOR THE
AIR IN MY LUNGS, THE NIGHT ALL AROUND ME.

⸸

_____

_____

_____

_____

_____

_____

_____

_____

_____

_____

_____

_____

_____

_____

_____

_____

_____

_____

_____

_____

_____

DATE _____

When was the last time you felt full of light?

Do you naturally prefer daylight or darkness? Why?

❖ 🌿 ❖

_____
_____
_____
_____
_____
_____
_____
_____
_____
_____
_____
_____
_____
_____
_____
_____
_____
_____
_____

DATE _____

IN TIME, SHE CAME TO THE BANKS OF A STREAM,
ITS SURFACE SO BRIGHT WITH STARLIGHT IT WAS AS IF
SOMEONE HAD PEELED THE RIND FROM THE MOON
LIKE A PIECE OF FRUIT AND LAID IT IN A GLEAMING
RIBBON UPON THE FOREST FLOOR.

DATE _____

Which phase or shape of the moon
is most magical to you? Why?

_____

_____

_____

_____

_____

_____

_____

_____

_____

_____

_____

_____

_____

_____

_____

_____

_____

_____

_____

_____

DATE _____

Write a story about capturing the moon.

THERE ARE DIFFERENT KINDS OF MAGIC. SOME CALL FOR RARE HERBS OR COMPLICATED INCANTATIONS. SOME DEMAND BLOOD. OTHER MAGIC IS MORE MYSTERIOUS STILL, THE KIND THAT FITS ONE VOICE TO ANOTHER, ONE BEING TO ANOTHER, WHEN MOMENTS BEFORE THEY WERE AS GOOD AS STRANGERS.

✦

DATE _____

Have you ever met someone and bonded immediately?
Describe it.

_____

_____

_____

_____

_____

_____

_____

_____

_____

_____

_____

_____

_____

_____

_____

_____

_____

_____

_____

_____

_____

DATE_____

MAYBE LOVE WAS SUPERSTITION, A PRAYER WE SAID
TO KEEP THE TRUTH OF LONELINESS AT BAY.

DATE

Do you believe in true love? What about love at first sight? Why or why not?

DATE_____

What kind of love do you value most—romantic?
Platonic? Familial? Love of self? Why?

_____

_____

_____

_____

_____

_____

_____

_____

_____

_____

_____

_____

_____

_____

_____

_____

_____

_____

_____

DATE _____

"Return with the beast's heart and all will pay you homage and you will want for nothing in this life," said the king. Ayama had no wish to be a princess. She had no wish to slay the beast.

DATE _____

What beast would you wish to slay?
What beast would you refuse to slay?

_____

_____

_____

_____

_____

_____

_____

_____

_____

_____

_____

_____

_____

_____

_____

_____

_____

_____

_____

_____

DATE _____

What is more important to you: duty or morality?

EVEN THAT FAINT TOUCH OPENED THE CONNECTION
BETWEEN US, AND A RUSH OF POWER VIBRATED
THROUGH ME LIKE A BELL BEING STRUCK.

DATE _____

Are there relationships in your life that
feel like magic? How so?

Describe your ideal mental or emotional
connection to another person.

_____

_____

_____

_____

_____

_____

_____

_____

_____

_____

_____

_____

_____

_____

_____

_____

_____

_____

_____

_____

_____

DATE _____

Describe your ideal physical connection to another person.

WE ALL KNOW THE STORY OF HOW THE QUEEN BECAME A QUEEN, HOW DESPITE HER TATTERED CLOTHES AND LOWLY POSITION, HER BEAUTY DREW THE NOTICE OF THE YOUNG PRINCE AND SHE WAS BROUGHT TO THE PALACE, WHERE SHE WAS DRESSED IN GOLD AND HER HAIR WAS WOVEN WITH JEWELS AND ALL WERE MADE TO KNEEL BEFORE A GIRL WHO HAD BEEN NOTHING BUT A SERVANT BARE DAYS BEFORE.

✦

DATE_____

Write your own story of a queen becoming a queen.

_____

_____

_____

_____

_____

_____

_____

_____

_____

_____

_____

_____

_____

_____

_____

_____

_____

_____

_____

_____

_____

_____

DATE_____

What do you think it would be like to be
an all-powerful ruler for a day?
What kind of ruler would you be?

✤✤✤ ✤✤✤

_____

_____

_____

_____

_____

_____

_____

_____

_____

_____

_____

_____

_____

_____

_____

_____

_____

_____

_____

_____

DATE _____

WE HAD EDGES SO JAGGED WE CUT EACH OTHER SOMETIMES, BUT AS I CURLED UP ON MY SIDE, THE WARMTH OF THE FIRE AT MY BACK, I FELT A RUSH OF GRATITUDE SO SWEET IT MADE MY THROAT ACHE.

DATE _____

Do you think it's necessary for some
relationships to have jagged edges? Why?

_____

_____

_____

_____

_____

_____

_____

_____

_____

_____

_____

_____

_____

_____

_____

_____

_____

_____

DATE _____

Which of your jagged edges, if any,
would you like to smooth out?

_____

_____

_____

_____

_____

_____

_____

_____

_____

_____

_____

_____

_____

_____

_____

_____

_____

_____

_____

_____

DATE _____

How do your sharp edges serve you?

_____

_____

_____

_____

_____

_____

_____

_____

_____

_____

_____

_____

_____

_____

_____

_____

_____

_____

_____

_____

_____

DATE _____

SHE WASN'T YET READY TO SPEAK THE DREAM THAT
HAD IGNITED IN HER HEART—A CREW OF HER OWN,
A SHIP UNDER HER COMMAND, A CRUSADE.

DATE

What do you dream of doing with your time?

_____

_____

_____

_____

_____

_____

_____

_____

_____

_____

_____

_____

_____

_____

_____

_____

_____

_____

_____

DATE _____

What did you dream of doing as a child?
What did you want to grow up to be?
Did your dreams change as you got older?

_____

_____

_____

_____

_____

_____

_____

_____

_____

_____

_____

_____

_____

_____

_____

_____

_____

_____

_____

_____

DATE _____

THEY PRAY THAT THEIR CHILDREN WILL BE BRAVE
AND CLEVER AND STRONG, THAT THEY WILL TELL THE
TRUE STORIES INSTEAD OF THE EASY ONES.

DATE _____

What is the difference between
a true story and an easy story?

DATE _____

Write a story that feels easy.
Rewrite the easy story to make it feel true.

THE BOY AND THE GIRL HAD ONCE DREAMED OF SHIPS,
LONG AGO, BEFORE THEY'D EVER SEEN THE TRUE SEA.
THEY WERE THE VESSELS OF STORIES, MAGIC SHIPS WITH
MASTS HEWN FROM SWEET CEDAR AND SAILS SPUN
BY MAIDENS FROM THREAD OF PURE GOLD.

DATE

Describe a vessel to carry you into sleep.

_____

_____

_____

_____

_____

_____

_____

_____

_____

_____

_____

_____

_____

_____

_____

_____

_____

_____

_____

_____

DATE _____

What makes for an ideal traveling companion?

Is there an imaginary world or landscape you
would like to live in or visit? Why?

_____

_____

_____

_____

_____

_____

_____

_____

_____

_____

_____

_____

_____

_____

_____

_____

_____

_____

_____

DATE_____

Describe a road trip through the last book
you read or film you watched.

_____

_____

_____

_____

_____

_____

_____

_____

_____

_____

_____

_____

_____

_____

_____

_____

_____

_____

_____

_____

_____

DATE _____

SHE'D NEVER FORGOTTEN THAT SENSE OF CONNECTION,
THE SUDDEN UNDERSTANDING THAT HER POWER
WOULD MEAN SHE WAS NEVER ALONE.

✦

DATE

How do you think power connects people
or separates them?

Do you prefer to be surrounded by people or left alone? Are you the same person in both situations? Why or why not?

❖ 🌿 ❖

_____

_____

_____

_____

_____

_____

_____

_____

_____

_____

_____

_____

_____

_____

_____

_____

_____

_____

_____

DATE_____

HE LOOKED AS IF HE'D FALLEN INTO
THE WRONG STORY, A PRINCE TURNED PAUPER.

DATE _____

Write the tale of a person in the wrong story.

_____

_____

_____

_____

_____

_____

_____

_____

_____

_____

_____

_____

_____

_____

_____

_____

_____

_____

_____

_____

DATE _____

WHEN THE WORLD OWED YOU NOTHING,
YOU DEMANDED SOMETHING OF IT ANYWAY.

DATE _____

What, if anything, does the world owe us?
What, if anything, do we owe the world?

_____

_____

_____

_____

_____

_____

_____

_____

_____

_____

_____

_____

_____

_____

_____

_____

_____

_____

_____

_____

DATE_____

What quality or trait do you most value
in the people around you?

"I DON'T HOLD A GRUDGE. I CRADLE IT. I CODDLE IT. I FEED IT FINE CUTS OF MEAT AND SEND IT TO THE BEST SCHOOLS. I NURTURE MY GRUDGES."

DATE _____

What is your longest-standing grudge or
a slight you've had trouble letting go?

DATE _____

Do you prefer to forgive and forget,
or to keep score? Why?

_____

_____

_____

_____

_____

_____

_____

_____

_____

_____

_____

_____

_____

_____

_____

_____

_____

_____

_____

DATE _____

Is there something you'd like to seek forgiveness for?
Ask for it here.

DATE _____

HE FELT AS IF HE'D LEFT SOME PART OF HIMSELF IN
THE COURTYARD BELOW, SOMETHING HE HADN'T
EVEN KNOWN MATTERED, INTANGIBLE AS MIST.

⟡

_____

_____

_____

_____

_____

_____

_____

_____

_____

_____

_____

_____

_____

_____

_____

_____

_____

_____

_____

_____

DATE_____

Think of an aspect of yourself you feel you've lost over time.
What would you need to reclaim it? Would you want to?

∞ ⟲ ∞

_____

_____

_____

_____

_____

_____

_____

_____

_____

_____

_____

_____

_____

_____

_____

_____

_____

_____

_____

_____

_____

Write a story about someone reclaiming
a missing part of themselves.

_____

_____

_____

_____

_____

_____

_____

_____

_____

_____

_____

_____

_____

_____

_____

_____

_____

_____

_____

_____

_____

DATE _____

"I WILL LOVE AN HONEST MONSTER BEFORE
I SWEAR LOYALTY TO A TREACHEROUS KING."

DATE _____

How do you define honesty, loyalty, and treachery?

_____
_____
_____
_____
_____
_____
_____
_____
_____
_____
_____
_____
_____
_____
_____
_____
_____
_____
_____
_____
_____

DATE _____

Do you value honesty or loyalty
more in the people around you?

Have you experienced betrayal?
How did you deal with it?

_____

_____

_____

_____

_____

_____

_____

_____

_____

_____

_____

_____

_____

_____

_____

_____

_____

_____

_____

_____

_____

DATE_____

SHE DID NOT KNOW WHAT TO CALL THE PLACE HE
BROUGHT HER TO. FAIRYLAND? THE LAND OF DREAMING?

_____

_____

_____

_____

_____

_____

_____

_____

_____

_____

_____

_____

_____

_____

_____

_____

_____

_____

_____

_____

_____

_____

_____

DATE_____

Describe the best dream you've ever had.

Create a guide to take you into the world of dreams.
Describe that person or creature here.

Is there a place you wish to visit? Can you incorporate
a symbol of that place into your daily life?

_____

_____

_____

_____

_____

_____

_____

_____

_____

_____

_____

_____

_____

_____

_____

_____

_____

DATE _____

"THANKS FOR FINDING ME."
I WASN'T SURE IF I WAS DREAMING, BUT SOMEWHERE IN
THE DARK, I THOUGHT I HEARD HIM WHISPER, "ALWAYS."

DATE _____

Who in your life do you turn to in times of need? Why?

Who would you drop everything to help? Why?

THE CRISP EDGE OF A WINTER WIND.
BARE BRANCHES. THE SMELL OF ABSENCE,
THE SMELL OF NIGHT.

DATE _____

How do you prepare for or celebrate winter?
Describe your perfect winter day.

_____

_____

_____

_____

_____

_____

_____

_____

_____

_____

_____

_____

_____

_____

_____

_____

_____

_____

_____

_____

DATE _____

Write a winter story.

_____

_____

_____

_____

_____

_____

_____

_____

_____

_____

_____

_____

_____

_____

_____

_____

_____

_____

_____

_____

DATE_____

THE WORLD TURNED GREEN THAT DAY, AND IT WAS
SAID THAT WHEREVER KIMA WENT YOU COULD SMELL
THE SWEET SCENT OF NEW GROWING THINGS.

How do you prepare for or celebrate spring?
Describe your perfect spring day.

_____

_____

_____

_____

_____

_____

_____

_____

_____

_____

_____

_____

_____

_____

_____

_____

_____

_____

DATE _____

Write a spring story.

DATE _____

"WHEN THE HEAT WAS AT ITS WORST, THEY ESCAPED
INTO THE WOODS TO HUNT FOR BIRDS' NESTS OR
SWIM IN THE MUDDY LITTLE CREEK, OR THEY WOULD
LIE FOR HOURS IN THEIR MEADOW, WATCHING
THE SUN PASS SLOWLY OVERHEAD . . ."

DATE

How do you prepare for or celebrate summer?
Describe your perfect summer day.

_____

_____

_____

_____

_____

_____

_____

_____

_____

_____

_____

_____

_____

_____

_____

_____

_____

_____

_____

_____

_____

DATE _____

Write a summer story.

_____

_____

_____

_____

_____

_____

_____

_____

_____

_____

_____

_____

_____

_____

_____

_____

_____

_____

_____

_____

DATE _____

THE AUTUMN LEAF MIGHT CLING TO ITS BRANCH,
BUT IT WAS ALREADY DEAD. THE ONLY QUESTION
WAS WHEN IT WOULD FALL.

DATE

How do you prepare for or celebrate autumn?
Describe your perfect autumn day.

_____

_____

_____

_____

_____

_____

_____

_____

_____

_____

_____

_____

_____

_____

_____

_____

_____

_____

_____

_____

DATE_____

Write an autumn story.

∞ ⟲ ∞

DATE _____

THE WORLD WAS MADE OF MIRACLES, UNEXPECTED
EARTHQUAKES, STORMS THAT CAME FROM NOWHERE
AND MIGHT RESHAPE A CONTINENT.

DATE _____

Describe a moment that changed the shape of your life.

_____

_____

_____

_____

_____

_____

_____

_____

_____

_____

_____

_____

_____

_____

_____

_____

_____

_____

_____

_____

DATE_____

If you could harness the power of any one force
of nature, what would it be and why?

_____

_____

_____

_____

_____

_____

_____

_____

_____

_____

_____

_____

_____

_____

_____

_____

_____

_____

_____

_____

_____

DATE _____

THE SEA SEEMED TO GO ON FOREVER, STRETCHING INTO
AN IMPOSSIBLY DISTANT HORIZON. I HAD SEEN PLENTY OF
MAPS. I KNEW THERE WAS LAND OUT THERE SOMEWHERE,
BEYOND LONG WEEKS OF TRAVEL AND MILES OF OCEAN.
BUT I STILL HAD THE DIZZYING SENSE THAT WE WERE
STANDING AT THE EDGE OF THE WORLD.

DATE _____

Describe a moment when you felt like you were standing on the edge of a new world or a frontier. Where were you?

_____

_____

_____

_____

_____

_____

_____

_____

_____

_____

_____

_____

_____

_____

_____

_____

_____

_____

_____

DATE _____

Write a story of a voyage, imaginary or real,
that moves between horizons.

_____

_____

_____

_____

_____

_____

_____

_____

_____

_____

_____

_____

_____

_____

_____

_____

_____

_____

_____

_____

_____

DATE _____

"WHEN SOMEONE DOES WRONG, WHEN WE MAKE
MISTAKES, WE DON'T SAY WE'RE SORRY.
WE PROMISE TO MAKE AMENDS."

⸎

_____

_____

_____

_____

_____

_____

_____

_____

_____

_____

_____

_____

_____

_____

_____

_____

_____

_____

_____

_____

_____

DATE_____

What is the difference between
apologizing and making amends?

DATE _____

Are there any amends you currently need to make?

＊＊＊ 🌹 ＊＊＊

_____

_____

_____

_____

_____

_____

_____

_____

_____

_____

_____

_____

_____

_____

_____

_____

_____

_____

_____

_____

_____

_____

_____

DATE _____

HE'D CAUGHT WITCHES; HOW DIFFERENT
COULD IT BE TO SLAY A DEMON?

DATE

Envision a problem you're having as
a monster or demon. Describe it.
In a story, how would you slay your demon?

_____
_____
_____
_____
_____
_____
_____
_____
_____
_____
_____
_____
_____
_____
_____
_____
_____
_____
_____
_____
_____
_____

THE GOWNS, THE JEWELS, THE CRYSTALS DRIPPING
FROM THE CHANDELIERS, EVEN THE FLOOR
BENEATH OUR FEET SEEMED TO SPARKLE.

DATE _____

Write the story of an enchanted ball.
Are you the protagonist or an observer?

_____
_____
_____
_____
_____
_____
_____
_____
_____
_____
_____
_____
_____
_____
_____
_____
_____
_____
_____
_____
_____
_____

Rewrite the story of yesterday's ball
from an opposing perspective.

✦ ☽ ✦

_____
_____
_____
_____
_____
_____
_____
_____
_____
_____
_____
_____
_____
_____
_____
_____
_____
_____
_____
_____
_____

DATE _____

"FOLLOW THE TALES OF WITCHES AND GOBLINS, AND UNEXPLAINED HAPPENINGS." SOMETIMES THEY WERE JUST SUPERSTITION. BUT OFTEN THERE WAS TRUTH AT THE HEART OF LOCAL LEGENDS.

❖

_____

_____

_____

_____

_____

_____

_____

_____

_____

_____

_____

_____

_____

_____

_____

_____

_____

_____

_____

_____

DATE_____

Describe a local legend or superstition that you heard growing up. What truth do you think lies at its heart?

_____

_____

_____

_____

_____

_____

_____

_____

_____

_____

_____

_____

_____

_____

_____

_____

_____

_____

_____

_____

DATE _____

Write a legend or superstition that embodies something important and true about the place where you live.

_____

_____

_____

_____

_____

_____

_____

_____

_____

_____

_____

_____

_____

_____

_____

_____

_____

_____

_____

DATE_____

MORE THAN ANY PLACE IN THE WORLD, THIS FELT
LIKE HOME TO HIM. BUT IT WAS HOME TURNED ON
ITS HEAD, HIS LIFE VIEWED AT THE WRONG ANGLE.

DATE

Describe a perfect place of refuge. How would you access it? Who would you allow inside?

_____

_____

_____

_____

_____

_____

_____

_____

_____

_____

_____

_____

_____

_____

_____

_____

_____

_____

DATE _____

What do you need around you to feel
at home in a new place?

_____
_____
_____
_____
_____
_____
_____
_____
_____
_____
_____
_____
_____
_____
_____
_____
_____
_____
_____
_____

DATE _____

ON THE HIGH WIRE, SHE WAS BEHOLDEN TO NO
ONE, A CREATURE WITHOUT PAST OR PRESENT,
SUSPENDED BETWEEN EARTH AND SKY.

_____

_____

_____

_____

_____

_____

_____

_____

_____

_____

_____

_____

_____

_____

_____

_____

_____

_____

_____

DATE_____

What would it mean to have no past or present?

Do you feel your actions and thoughts are
more shaped by your past or your present?

_____

_____

_____

_____

_____

_____

_____

_____

_____

_____

_____

_____

_____

_____

_____

_____

_____

_____

_____

DATE _____

"IN HER SLEEP, YOUR MOTHER SWALLOWED A BIT OF
NIGHT SKY, AND ALL OF THAT EMPTY IS STILL INSIDE YOU."

∞ ∞

DATE _____

What gifts and debts do you think you've
inherited from your parents?

_____

_____

_____

_____

_____

_____

_____

_____

_____

_____

_____

_____

_____

_____

_____

_____

_____

_____

_____

_____

DATE _____

THE HEART IS AN ARROW. IT DEMANDS AIM TO LAND TRUE.

DATE

Name one of your desires or ambitions.
Do you have a plan to achieve it?

_____

_____

_____

_____

_____

_____

_____

_____

_____

_____

_____

_____

_____

_____

_____

_____

_____

_____

DATE _____

Write a story about bad aim.

What lie would you never want to be told?

DATE _____

THE FIREBIRD WEPT DIAMOND TEARS, ITS FEATHERS
COULD HEAL MORTAL WOUNDS, THE FUTURE MIGHT
BE SEEN IN THE FLAP OF ITS WINGS.

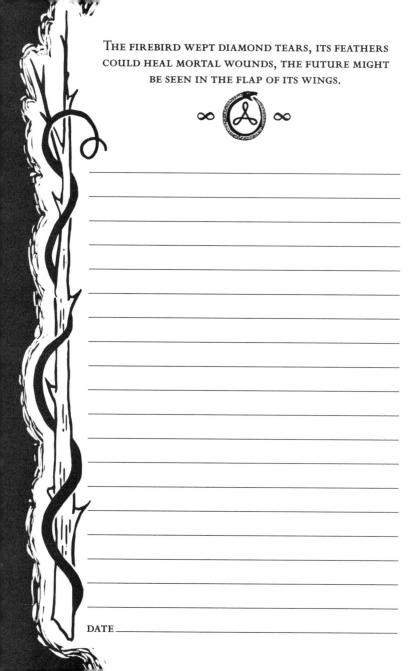

DATE

Describe a legendary creature with powers of healing.
Where is it found? What does it look like?
What wounds does it heal?
Describe a quest to find that creature.

❖

_____

_____

_____

_____

_____

_____

_____

_____

_____

_____

_____

_____

_____

_____

_____

_____

_____

_____

_____

_____

_____

DATE _____

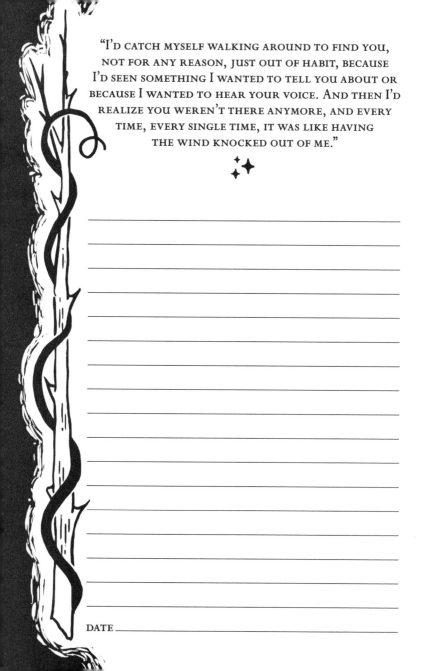

"I'D CATCH MYSELF WALKING AROUND TO FIND YOU,
NOT FOR ANY REASON, JUST OUT OF HABIT, BECAUSE
I'D SEEN SOMETHING I WANTED TO TELL YOU ABOUT OR
BECAUSE I WANTED TO HEAR YOUR VOICE. AND THEN I'D
REALIZE YOU WEREN'T THERE ANYMORE, AND EVERY
TIME, EVERY SINGLE TIME, IT WAS LIKE HAVING
THE WIND KNOCKED OUT OF ME."

DATE

Think of someone or something you've taken
for granted and write a thank-you here.

_____

_____

_____

_____

_____

_____

_____

_____

_____

_____

_____

_____

_____

_____

_____

_____

_____

_____

_____

_____

DATE_____

Who do you miss? What do you wish you
could share with that person?

_____

_____

_____

_____

_____

_____

_____

_____

_____

_____

_____

_____

_____

_____

_____

_____

_____

_____

_____

_____

DATE _____

THIS WAS HIS SOUL MADE FLESH, THE TRUTH
OF HIM LAID BARE IN THE BLAZING SUN,
SHORN OF MYSTERY AND SHADOW.

_____

_____

_____

_____

_____

_____

_____

_____

_____

_____

_____

_____

_____

_____

_____

_____

_____

_____

_____

_____

_____

_____

DATE _____

Can you ever fully know the truth of someone?
Why or why not?

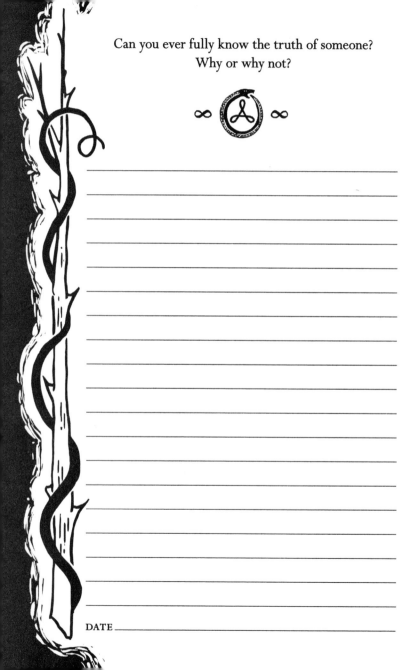

DATE _____

Do you have someone in your life who knows
you completely? Why or why not?

_____

_____

_____

_____

_____

_____

_____

_____

_____

_____

_____

_____

_____

_____

_____

_____

_____

_____

_____

_____

DATE _____

THEY HAD AN ORDINARY LIFE, FULL OF ORDINARY
THINGS—IF LOVE CAN EVER BE CALLED THAT.

DATE

Explain why you see love as ordinary or extraordinary.

⚜ 🌹 ⚜

_____
_____
_____
_____
_____
_____
_____
_____
_____
_____
_____
_____
_____
_____
_____
_____
_____
_____
_____
_____
_____

DATE _____

How do you define love?

DATE _____

Describe a time when you mistook something else for love.

_____

_____

_____

_____

_____

_____

_____

_____

_____

_____

_____

_____

_____

_____

_____

_____

_____

_____

_____

_____

_____

DATE_____

"Do you wish to become a monster?"

∞ 🐍 ∞

DATE

List three monsters from fairy tales or horror stories.
What do they symbolize? Why are they shown in this form?

❖ 🌿 ❖

_____

_____

_____

_____

_____

_____

_____

_____

_____

_____

_____

_____

_____

_____

_____

_____

_____

_____

_____

DATE_____

Describe a monster or a villain you've felt sympathy for.

_____

_____

_____

_____

_____

_____

_____

_____

_____

_____

_____

_____

_____

_____

_____

_____

_____

_____

_____

_____

_____

_____

_____

DATE_____

What monster would you permanently vanquish if you could?

_____

_____

_____

_____

_____

_____

_____

_____

_____

_____

_____

_____

_____

_____

_____

_____

_____

_____

_____

_____

DATE_____

HE STOPPED WORRYING ABOUT SEEMING NORMAL,
LET PEOPLE SEE A GLIMMER OF THE MADNESS
WITHIN HIM AND LET THEM GUESS AT THE REST.

DATE

Have you ever wanted to seem "normal"?
What did that mean to you?

_____
_____
_____
_____
_____
_____
_____
_____
_____
_____
_____
_____
_____
_____
_____
_____
_____
_____
_____

DATE _____

What parts of yourself do you like to keep hidden?

SHE'D MADE MEN FALL IN LOVE WITH HER BEFORE, WHEN SHE
WAS YOUNG AND CRUEL AND LIKED TO TEST HER POWER.

❖ 🌿 ❖

_____

_____

_____

_____

_____

_____

_____

_____

_____

_____

_____

_____

_____

_____

_____

_____

_____

_____

DATE _____

Can your heart be anything but your own?
Can another person's heart be yours? Why or why not?

_____
_____
_____
_____
_____
_____
_____
_____
_____
_____
_____
_____
_____
_____
_____
_____
_____
_____
_____
_____

DATE _____

THEY WERE ALL DECEIVERS AND SPIES,
TRAINED TO PREY ON PEOPLE LIKE HIM, PEOPLE
WITHOUT THEIR UNNATURAL GIFTS.

_____

DATE _____

Do you feel that you are predator or prey? Describe a situation when you've felt like a hunter or the hunted.

_____

_____

_____

_____

_____

_____

_____

_____

_____

_____

_____

_____

_____

_____

_____

_____

_____

_____

_____

_____

DATE _____

What unnatural gifts would you like to claim?

_____

_____

_____

_____

_____

_____

_____

_____

_____

_____

_____

_____

_____

_____

_____

_____

_____

_____

_____

_____

DATE_____

THE STORY NEEDED AN ENDING THAT WAS TRUE.

What does it take for a happy ending to feel true?

✦ 🌿 ✦

_____

_____

_____

_____

_____

_____

_____

_____

_____

_____

_____

_____

_____

_____

_____

_____

_____

_____

_____

DATE_____

THEY WERE LIKE ANYONE ELSE. FULL OF THE POTENTIAL TO DO GREAT GOOD, AND ALSO GREAT HARM.

DATE _____

What do you think is your greatest potential to do good?

_____
_____
_____
_____
_____
_____
_____
_____
_____
_____
_____
_____
_____
_____
_____
_____
_____
_____
_____
_____

DATE _____

What do you think is your greatest potential to do harm?

_____

_____

_____

_____

_____

_____

_____

_____

_____

_____

_____

_____

_____

_____

_____

_____

_____

_____

_____

_____

DATE_____

HER HEART FELT TOO FULL, A DRY CREEK
BED ILL-PREPARED FOR SUCH RAIN.

_____

_____

_____

_____

_____

_____

_____

_____

_____

_____

_____

_____

_____

_____

_____

_____

_____

_____

_____

DATE _____

Describe a moment when you were
overwhelmed by an emotion.

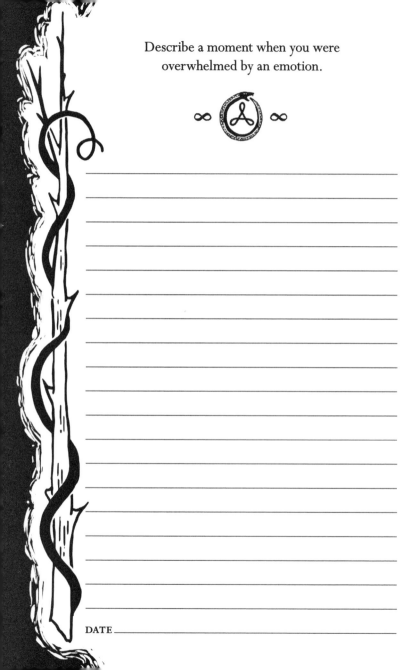

DATE

Write a story about the end of a drought.

_____

_____

_____

_____

_____

_____

_____

_____

_____

_____

_____

_____

_____

_____

_____

_____

_____

_____

_____

_____

DATE_____

SOME PRESSED LITTLE GIFTS ON US, THE ONLY OFFERINGS
THEY HAD: HOARDED BREAD ROLLS GONE TOOTH-
BREAKINGLY HARD, POLISHED STONES, BITS OF LACE,
A CLUTCH OF SALT LILIES. THEY MURMURED PRAYERS
FOR OUR HEALTH WITH TEARS IN THEIR EYES.

DATE

How do you define generosity?

_____

_____

_____

_____

_____

_____

_____

_____

_____

_____

_____

_____

_____

_____

_____

_____

_____

_____

_____

_____

_____

DATE _____

Describe a gift you've received that felt like a burden.

HER MIND REFUSED THE IMAGE BEFORE HER. THIS COULD
NOT BE REAL. IT WAS AN ILLUSION, A FALSE REFLECTION,
A LIE MADE IN RAINBOW-HUED GLASS.

DATE

When have you experienced something you
feared was too good to be true? Was it?

_____

_____

_____

_____

_____

_____

_____

_____

_____

_____

_____

_____

_____

_____

_____

_____

_____

_____

_____

_____

_____

DATE _____

Are there illusions that you would like
to create and keep for yourself?

_____

_____

_____

_____

_____

_____

_____

_____

_____

_____

_____

_____

_____

_____

_____

_____

_____

_____

_____

_____

DATE_____

YOU LIVE IN A SINGLE MOMENT. I LIVE IN A THOUSAND.

DATE

Write a story about an immortal.

_____
_____
_____
_____
_____
_____
_____
_____
_____
_____
_____
_____
_____
_____
_____
_____
_____
_____
_____
_____
_____
_____

DATE_____

HE'D NEVER LIKED THE OCEAN, THE SENSE OF THE UNKNOWN BENEATH HIS FEET, THAT SOMETHING HUNGRY AND FULL OF TEETH MIGHT BE WAITING TO DRAG HIM UNDER. AND THAT WAS HOW HE FELT EVERY DAY NOW, EVEN ON LAND.

DATE

Describe a time you felt threatened or
exhilarated by the unknown.

_____

_____

_____

_____

_____

_____

_____

_____

_____

_____

_____

_____

_____

_____

_____

_____

_____

_____

_____

_____

DATE _____

Is there something "hungry and full of teeth" you feel
the need to guard against? How do you protect yourself?

Do you seek out experiences that frighten you?
Why or why not?

_____

_____

_____

_____

_____

_____

_____

_____

_____

_____

_____

_____

_____

_____

_____

_____

_____

_____

_____

_____

_____

DATE_____

FEAR IS A PHOENIX. YOU CAN WATCH IT BURN
A THOUSAND TIMES AND STILL IT WILL RETURN.

DATE

Do you think fear is useful?
Why or why not?

_____

_____

_____

_____

_____

_____

_____

_____

_____

_____

_____

_____

_____

_____

_____

_____

_____

_____

_____

_____

_____

_____

DATE_____

What are your fears?

DATE _____

Write the opposite of each of your fears here—
imagine turning each one into a strength.

_____

_____

_____

_____

_____

_____

_____

_____

_____

_____

_____

_____

_____

_____

_____

_____

_____

_____

_____

_____

DATE_____

HE SENT HOME A PACKET OF TEA THAT MADE A FLOWER BLOOM BENEATH THE DRINKER'S TONGUE; ANOTHER THAT, WHEN SIPPED BEFORE BEDTIME, ASSURED YOU WOULD DREAM OF THE CITY OF YOUR BIRTH; AND A BLEND SO BITTER ONE SIP WOULD MAKE YOU CRY FOR THREE HOURS.

DATE

What flavors do you find most powerful or transporting?

❖ 🌿 ❖

_____

_____

_____

_____

_____

_____

_____

_____

_____

_____

_____

_____

_____

_____

_____

_____

_____

_____

_____

_____

_____

DATE _____

Tell the story of someone brewing you a magical cup of tea.

_____
_____
_____
_____
_____
_____
_____
_____
_____
_____
_____
_____
_____
_____
_____
_____
_____
_____
_____
_____
_____

DATE _____

"STOP TREATING YOUR PAIN LIKE IT'S SOMETHING YOU IMAGINED. IF YOU SEE THE WOUND IS REAL, THEN YOU CAN HEAL IT."

_____

_____

_____

_____

_____

_____

_____

_____

_____

_____

_____

_____

_____

_____

_____

_____

_____

_____

_____

DATE _____

Do you admit to pain when you suffer it?
Why or why not?

_____

_____

_____

_____

_____

_____

_____

_____

_____

_____

_____

_____

_____

_____

_____

_____

_____

_____

_____

_____

_____

_____

DATE _____

Write a story about acknowledging and healing pain.

IT WAS EASY TO BELIEVE THAT IZUMRUD STILL LIVED
SOMEWHERE, WAITING TO BE WOKEN BY THE CALL OF
HEROES . . . A BEAST LIKE THAT RESTS; HE DOES NOT DIE.

DATE _____

What would it mean to rest but never die?

_____

_____

_____

_____

_____

_____

_____

_____

_____

_____

_____

_____

_____

_____

_____

_____

_____

_____

_____

DATE _____

A THOUSAND DESPERATE WISHES HAVE BEEN
SPOKEN ON THESE SHORES, AND IN THE END THEY
ARE ALL THE SAME: *MAKE ME SOMEONE NEW.*

DATE _____

If you could spend a day as someone
else, who would it be?

_____

_____

_____

_____

_____

_____

_____

_____

_____

_____

_____

_____

_____

_____

_____

_____

_____

_____

_____

_____

DATE _____

If you could change one thing
about yourself, what would it be?

_____

_____

_____

_____

_____

_____

_____

_____

_____

_____

_____

_____

_____

_____

_____

_____

_____

_____

_____

DATE _____

What was the last thing you wished for?
What did you do to make it real?

_____

_____

_____

_____

_____

_____

_____

_____

_____

_____

_____

_____

_____

_____

_____

_____

_____

_____

_____

_____

DATE _____

DO YOU FEEL THAT? THE TEACHER ASKED.
*ALL YOUR HEARTS, BEATING IN SHARED TIME, BOUND
TO THE RHYTHM OF THE WORLD?*

DATE

Describe a way in which all humans are connected.

❖ 🌿 ❖

_____

_____

_____

_____

_____

_____

_____

_____

_____

_____

_____

_____

_____

_____

_____

_____

_____

_____

DATE _____

Listen for a moment.
Describe three things you hear.

"THERE IS NO MAGIC THAT CAN MAKE THEM LOVE YOU."

_____

_____

_____

_____

_____

_____

_____

_____

_____

_____

_____

_____

_____

_____

_____

_____

_____

_____

_____

DATE _____

When have you felt heartbroken?
Describe the story of your first heartbreak.

Would you cast a love spell if you could?
Why or why not?

_____

_____

_____

_____

_____

_____

_____

_____

_____

_____

_____

_____

_____

_____

_____

_____

_____

_____

_____

_____

DATE _____

Write a story about love compelled by magic.

HERE THE TREES SPARKED WITH FIREFLIES AND
THE SKY WAS THE CLOUDY PURPLE OF A RIPE PLUM.
SHE HAD REACHED THE HEART OF THE WOOD.

_____

_____

_____

_____

_____

_____

_____

_____

_____

_____

_____

_____

_____

_____

_____

_____

_____

_____

_____

_____

DATE_____

Do you have an affinity for any particular color? What is it?
Is there a color you dislike particularly? Why?

_____

_____

_____

_____

_____

_____

_____

_____

_____

_____

_____

_____

_____

_____

_____

_____

_____

_____

_____

_____

DATE _____

Twilight is a time of transition. How does
your mood change from day to night?

_____

_____

_____

_____

_____

_____

_____

_____

_____

_____

_____

_____

_____

_____

_____

_____

_____

_____

_____

_____

_____

_____

DATE _____

"THERE IS A GREAT DIFFERENCE BETWEEN NOT
EATING A PERSON AND TRUSTING A PERSON."

DATE _____

Whom do you trust and why?
How does a person earn your trust?

_____

_____

_____

_____

_____

_____

_____

_____

_____

_____

_____

_____

_____

_____

_____

_____

_____

_____

_____

_____

DATE _____

THEY WERE ALL SEARCHING THE PAGES OF HUMAN
BOOKS FOR MORTAL MAGIC . . . THE THING THAT
MIGHT CHANGE THEIR FORTUNES FOREVER.

∞ ∞

DATE _____

Write the story of a quest undertaken by a non-mortal
creature in our everyday human world.

❖ 🌿 ❖

_____

_____

_____

_____

_____

_____

_____

_____

_____

_____

_____

_____

_____

_____

_____

_____

_____

_____

_____

_____

DATE_____

THERE WERE TONICS AND OINTMENTS, BITTER-
SMELLING PASTES, JEWEL-COLORED POWDERS PACKED
IN SMALL ENAMEL BOXES, TINCTURES IN BROWN
GLASS BOTTLES. THERE WAS ALWAYS SOMETHING
STRANGE BREWING ON THAT STOVE.

DATE

Start a shelf of things that inspire you or feel powerful to you. What is on it? What is still to be acquired?

_____

_____

_____

_____

_____

_____

_____

_____

_____

_____

_____

_____

_____

_____

_____

_____

_____

_____

_____

_____

DATE _____

What is your most precious talisman?

HEALING WAS SLOW, DELIBERATE, A RHYTHM THAT
REQUIRED THOUGHTFUL STUDY OF EACH SMALL CHOICE.

DATE _____

What choices do people need to make in order to heal?

Hurt and healing often go together. Describe
a time when you experienced one or both.

_____

_____

_____

_____

_____

_____

_____

_____

_____

_____

_____

_____

_____

_____

_____

_____

_____

_____

_____

DATE _____

What would you heal in yourself now?

DATE _____

BETTER THAN ANYONE, SHE KNEW THE
POWER OF THINGS LONG BURIED.

_____

_____

_____

_____

_____

_____

_____

_____

_____

_____

_____

_____

_____

_____

_____

_____

_____

_____

_____

_____

DATE _____

Are there things that should stay buried?
What are they?

_____
_____
_____
_____
_____
_____
_____
_____
_____
_____
_____
_____
_____
_____
_____
_____
_____
_____
_____
_____
_____
_____
_____

DATE _____

Are there things that should be brought into the light?
What are they?

_____

_____

_____

_____

_____

_____

_____

_____

_____

_____

_____

_____

_____

_____

_____

_____

_____

_____

_____

_____

DATE_____

SHE TOLD THE STUDENTS PECULIAR STORIES OF FLYING SHIPS AND UNDERGROUND CASTLES, OF MONSTERS WHO ATE EARTH, AND BIRDS THAT ROSE ON WINGS OF FLAME.

∞ ⦵ ∞

DATE

Describe your ideal imaginary landscape.

_____

_____

_____

_____

_____

_____

_____

_____

_____

_____

_____

_____

_____

_____

_____

_____

_____

_____

_____

_____

_____

DATE _____

If you could communicate with a wild animal or
imagined creature, what would you say to each other?
Describe that encounter.

_____

_____

_____

_____

_____

_____

_____

_____

_____

_____

_____

_____

_____

_____

_____

_____

_____

_____

_____

_____

_____

DATE _____

HER LIFE HAD BEEN A SERIES OF IMPOSSIBLE MOMENTS,
SO WHY NOT ASK FOR SOMETHING IMPOSSIBLE NOW?

DATE

What "impossible" moments have you
encountered in your life?

_____

_____

_____

_____

_____

_____

_____

_____

_____

_____

_____

_____

_____

_____

_____

_____

_____

_____

_____

_____

_____

DATE _____

What "impossible" thing would you most like to have?

EVERYTHING MADE SENSE. THEIR BODIES WERE A MAP OF
CELLS, A THOUSAND EQUATIONS, SOLVED BY THE SECOND,
BY THE MILLISECOND, AND SHE KNEW ONLY ANSWERS.

What has been your moment of greatest
understanding or revelation?

_____

_____

_____

_____

_____

_____

_____

_____

_____

_____

_____

_____

_____

_____

_____

_____

_____

_____

_____

_____

DATE _____

Do you think magic and science are separate or linked?
Why or why not?

DATE _____

THE RIVER LAUGHED AT HIS JOKES, LISTENED AND
MURMURED ASSENT, ROARED IN SHARED ANGER
AND INDIGNATION WHEN HE'D BEEN WRONGED.

_____

_____

_____

_____

_____

_____

_____

_____

_____

_____

_____

_____

_____

_____

_____

_____

_____

_____

_____

_____

DATE_____

Describe the experience of swimming in
or being carried along by a river.

_____

_____

_____

_____

_____

_____

_____

_____

_____

_____

_____

_____

_____

_____

_____

_____

_____

_____

_____

_____

DATE _____

Write a story about something in nature
trying to communicate.

_____

_____

_____

_____

_____

_____

_____

_____

_____

_____

_____

_____

_____

_____

_____

_____

_____

_____

_____

_____

DATE_____

If you had to choose between a life underground, a life underwater, or a life only in the air, which would it be and why?

BUT THEY WERE HIS FIRST FRIENDS, HIS ONLY FRIENDS . . .
EVEN IF HE'D HAD HIS PICK OF A THOUSAND COMPANIONS,
THESE WOULD HAVE BEEN THE PEOPLE HE CHOSE.

❖ 🌿 ❖

_____

_____

_____

_____

_____

_____

_____

_____

_____

_____

_____

_____

_____

_____

_____

_____

_____

_____

_____

_____

_____

DATE_____

Have you ever found a friend when you needed one most?
How did they support you?

_____

_____

_____

_____

_____

_____

_____

_____

_____

_____

_____

_____

_____

_____

_____

_____

_____

_____

_____

_____

_____

_____

DATE _____

Have you provided that support for someone else?

✿

DATE

WASN'T THAT WHAT EVERY GIRL DREAMED? THAT SHE'D
WAKE AND FIND HERSELF A PRINCESS? OR BLESSED WITH
MAGICAL POWERS AND A GRAND DESTINY? MAYBE
THERE WERE PEOPLE WHO LIVED THOSE LIVES.

DATE

Whose life would you choose to wake
up in other than your own?

_____

_____

_____

_____

_____

_____

_____

_____

_____

_____

_____

_____

_____

_____

_____

_____

_____

_____

_____

_____

DATE _____

Write the story of your own life as a fairy tale.

THE DREAMS WERE THE ONLY PLACE IT WAS SAFE TO
USE HER POWER NOW, AND SHE LONGED FOR THEM.

❖ 🌿 ❖

_____

_____

_____

_____

_____

_____

_____

_____

_____

_____

_____

_____

_____

_____

_____

_____

_____

_____

_____

_____

DATE_____

Are there powers you've had in your dreams
that you wish you could use in real life?

Describe a magical power you would not wish to have.

‐‐‐ ❀ ‐‐‐

_____

_____

_____

_____

_____

_____

_____

_____

_____

_____

_____

_____

_____

_____

_____

_____

_____

_____

_____

_____

DATE _____

ON THE KITCHEN TABLE LAY AN OVERTURNED BOTTLE OF
WINE AND THE REMNANTS OF WHAT MUST HAVE BEEN A
CAKE, THE CRUMBS STILL SCENTED WITH ORANGE BLOSSOM.

_____

_____

_____

_____

_____

_____

_____

_____

_____

_____

_____

_____

_____

_____

_____

_____

_____

_____

_____

_____

DATE _____

If you could prepare any meal for your
favorite person, what would it be and why?

_____

_____

_____

_____

_____

_____

_____

_____

_____

_____

_____

_____

_____

_____

_____

_____

_____

_____

_____

DATE_____

I AM BECOME A BLADE.

If you could be a weapon to make change, what kind of weapon would you be and what kind of change would you make?

_____

_____

_____

_____

_____

_____

_____

_____

_____

_____

_____

_____

_____

_____

_____

_____

_____

_____

_____

DATE _____

I WAS THE WITCH IN THE WOOD, THE QUEEN
ON HER THRONE, THE GODDESS IN HER TEMPLE.

DATE

What are the different roles you play in your life?

_____

_____

_____

_____

_____

_____

_____

_____

_____

_____

_____

_____

_____

_____

_____

_____

_____

_____

_____

DATE _____

When are you at your most powerful?

"MAGIC DOESN'T REQUIRE BEAUTY," SHE SAID. "EASY MAGIC IS PRETTY. GREAT MAGIC ASKS THAT YOU TROUBLE THE WATERS. IT REQUIRES A DISRUPTION, SOMETHING NEW."

DATE

Write a story about creating a new, great magic.